Stairs to the Top

Seneca Wilson

A collection of poems to motivate the world to
Give More Love

SenecaTMPoet | Jackson, MS

Seneca Wilson/SenecaTMPoet Publishing
Jackson, MS
www.senecatmpoet.com

Book cover © multiimagesgraphics.com
Edited by Mozart Guerrier
Foreword by Gemineye The Poet

Stairs to the Top/ Seneca Wilson. -- 1st ed.
ISBN 978-0-692-63497-4

Also by Seneca Wilson | Kind of a One

This book is dedicated to my wife, Meghan and son, Tylan. Love is the greatest gift, so I encourage you to always Give More Love in everything you do.

"Luck is what happens when preparation meets opportunity."

–SENECA THE YOUNGER

He took the elevator,
she took the escalator,
and I took the stairs to the top.
When I arrive,
I won't come back down for a long time,
because I know how many steps I took to get here.

Contents

FOREWORD

Seneca!
Hopeful
Confident
Optimistic
Positive
Cheerful
Sanguine
Upbeat
Encouraging
Propitious
Auspicious
Motivational
Seneca is a motivational poet
Seneca, THE Motivational Poet
Know it
Embrace it
Embrace the energy
Be free
Be
Be everything you ever wanted to be
And then be more
Explore
Move past your inhibitions
Multiply your optimism
The instructions to better your life can be found inside
    this booklet
Don't just thumb through it

Do it.
These pages will spcak to you.
They will speak your courage into existence
Resistance is futile
Take the STAIRS TO THE TOP.
Non-stop
This book is your guide
The ride is unimaginable
Tap your unknown potential
Let Seneca be your guide
He is inspiring
He is masterful
He is motivational
He is art
Let art imitate life
Because art can dictate life
So let this art dictate your life
Put one foot in front of the other
And thumb through the pages
Be creative
And state this: "I CAN succeed!"
I can give more love!
I can be love
And I can be loved
All is love
I am love
Love is motivation
Creation starts with love
And success is the fruit of that labor
Wager on yourself

Bet on your benevolence
Be a spectacle of amazing embracing
Hug often
Be supported
Be supportive
Be forward
You're gorgeous
And everything about you is worth being praised
This book is an introduction into who you ought to
    aspire to be
So read
Dedicate yourself to this text
And flex your heart
Because Seneca's art
Can take you where you need to go
All you need to know
Is where to start.
So start, here.

Unfinished Poem

They say a poet should never read an unfinished poem,
but I will read this anyway
Because if the words on the page are alive when spoken
what poem is ever finished?
The author of this poem
is the greatest poet you will ever know.
He has been writing miracles for many years
This poem is meant to heal, inspire,
motivate the soul to give more love.
This poem is LOVE!

And this poem is not finished
It is still being written, revised, workshopped, and
edited
for you...
Hoping that one day
this poem may eventually inspire your life
like a masterpiece before its true beauty,
an idea before it's executed,
this poem is written for you, you, you, you, and you
to be placed in your heart,
carried in your soul,
a daily motivation,
and hopefully the greatest poem you will ever know

And even though it is not finished
I...Am...A...Poem!

I hope that we cross paths when you really need me
let my words be sweet symphonies in your ear
like your favorite love song you hear on
Sunday morning.
I want to be an unexpected gift on Christmas Eve,
an incandescent angel hanging from a tree,
allow me to be the light in your life.
I want to be your messenger of love,
the one you trust with your skeletons,
and your elephants can roam free in my home
There is no judgment here
only medicine for the soul to heal, inspire,
motivate the soul to give more love
I...Am...Love!

And I am not finished
I have so much more love to give
I want to be your soil,
your sun,
your rain,
your whatever it takes to make you grow
I want to be your right now
I don't want to wait until tomorrow
I want to live in your moments,
because moments are the only thing that really matters
I want to be a poem for you
not a poem you memorize,

but a poem you know,
because the mind is fragilc and forgetful sometimes
I want to find a vacant space in your heart to dwell in
your memories,
so you can rely on me
when you need a poem to make you smile
I...Am...Your...Poem!

And I am not finished
I am still being written...

18,632 Days

-Inspired by Dr. Dennis Kimbro

You have 18,632 days left on this earth
    what are you going to do with the rest of them?
    While you sit there and contemplate life
    the earth is constantly spinning on its axis,
    and time stops for no one.
    Are you going to let these days, these hours, these
    minutes just pass you by?
    Because if you want something
    go get it!
    Wake up to life with a purpose,
    knowing that the morning never escapes the sun
    and allow determination to creep through your blinds
    to remind you
that hope will be waiting for you at your door step.
    So, walk with confidence
    hand in hand with faith
    placing one foot in front of the next
    not knowing if these steps will be your last,
    but be willing to die to get it right this time.
    I want you to live with passion!
    Leave your legacy behind for someone to find your
    footsteps to greatness
    Remember there is no success without sacrifice,

and more doors will close than open,
and always be prepared for an opportunity.
So, fight for what you want
because success is only inches, moments, or seconds
away
Take risks and stand up for want you want!
Do it now!
Right now!
Because you have 18,632 days left on this earth.
What are you going to do with the rest of them?

A wise man once said,

"People become what they eat."

I Am Poetry!

Belle

I can still taste the Montrachet Chardonnay on the
tip of her lips

as if...
she was preserved to be as fine as she is...
She is...from Burgundy
with an accent so deep,
as rich as the Gâteaux soufflé she was eating
It's intriguing how her smile resembles a split
image of the French Riviera,

and I swear her Côte d' Azur is elegant and
sophisticated...
and my eyes are hypnotized as they follow along
the border of her coastline.
I swear to you
she is that beautiful
Tall...
like the Eiffel Tower
and her hair hangs down the back of her neck like
the Gavarnie Falls
something like Noémie Lenoir in Rush Hour.
Yes!

She is that beautiful
Belle...

I adore how she smells exactly like Paris
Her Chanel Coco Mademoiselle fragrance is
alluring,

and I am indulged as she leaned over and
whispered to me,
"J'adore ta façon de t' addresser a' moi
Je vous te baiser."
And then....
she kissed me,
and I can still taste the Montrachet Chardonnay on
the tip of her lips,

as if she was preserved to be as fine as she is...
She is...Belle

Give More Love

Love is the most powerful thing that has ever lived,
    and just like Shakespeare
    I want to record our love,
    so when this world ends
    in the next book of Genesis
    Adam and Eve would stumble over our work
    instead of the sweet apple of sin, and
    understand that this is the way we were meant
    to be.
They would create children based on our theory,
    and the 10 commandments would go something
    like this:

    Love our father
He is the creator of all things
He is love and through love all things are possible

    Love thy self
Because you are a pure image of God
An angel personally picked from God's garden,
as a gift to bless the earth with your presence

    Love thy family
Because family is a full circle,

and a man is merely a bone with an incomplete
    skeleton
in search to find the perfect rib
to produce more seeds to the earth

    Love to live
Live life to the fullest,
as if the sun never set
the ocean never ends,
and understand that there are more possibilities
    beyond the galaxy

    Love to give
as God gave to the earth
unselfishly
because a man should never be asked to give,
as for the gift should be asked to be received

    Love to laugh
Because laughter is the wind behind the clouds,
medicine for the soul,
and the summer of all seasons
it allows you to get through life

    Love to cry
as if you are a waterfall
allow your tears to cleanse the heart,
so that joy will be manifested in the soul,

and the sun will bring brighter days

 Love to dream
Because dreams are the possibilities of reality,
and when you are allowed to dream
you create the future

 Love to forgive
Because man is created equally,
and mistakes are only life learned lessons
in order for your flower to blossom

 Love to work
Because you are made of the earth,
and just like the earth
you have many precious stones and jewels buried
 deep inside,
but you must search and dig deep,
as gold miners in order to find your fortune

 Yes, our love will be recorded and left behind
 for someone to find the greatest gift you can
 give,
 and it is a shame we don't all have presents
 because it is like water to plants
 it makes the earth spin on its axis.
 Love is exactly what the world needs
 So, just like our Father from above
 You should always Give More Love!

I wrap myself
in our covers
when you are not around,
so I can smell
your fragrance
marinated in our sheets

Oral Language

The oral language is the most misunderstood
form of communication because we don't take
the time to understand and interpret

that everybody is looking for the same things
They just have different ways of expressing it,
and because we don't all speak the same
language we stay divided

According to book of genesis
one language is the key to all things

Nothing is impossible if we are all in unity
but wait, we do communicate in one
language...actions!
Somebody said actions speak louder than
words,
but I say actions speak to who you are.
I have seen elephants care for their young like
my wife with a newborn
Bees fight for their queen like we fight for our

country
You see, oral language is misunderstood until
we listen

I said, oral language is misunderstood until we
listen...like poetry
Whether it is in English, Latin, French, or Spanish
We all understand love, protection, smiles,
frowns, joy...
Actions are everything,
and without it
It's like faith without God...meaningless
We need to communicate like black and white
keys

   playing in perfect harmony.
   Can you imagine how beautiful this world
   would be...

She is my Medicine

She is my medicine
She is my medicine
She is my Geodon
My Ativan
My IV
My Sudafed
She makes me feel good...uh!

She is my love deity
The birth of Venus's daughter
Her love flows like water into the sea of my
mouth,

and I swallow her...whole.
Arousing my endorphins
her love is like sea dolphins,
and she keeps me high
off of her intelligence
gives me opiates from her elegance,
and her taste
makes me feel good...uh!

She is my medicine
She is my medicine
She is my Geodon
My Ativan
My IV
My Sudafed
She makes me feel good...uh!

I admit, I am addicted
to the way heaven sits on her lips,
and how her rainbow kisses taste like honey
It's funny, how she is the beat to my rhythm,

and her heart plays my favorite tune
Like with each heartbeat
I fall...deeper...in love...with her
into a drunken stupor,
and some days I try to go sober
just so I can relapse
like Amy Winehouse
Forget rehab!
(I say no no no)
I want to die
just...like...this
in love
with her
because she makes me feel good...uh!

She is my medicine
She is my medicine
She is my Geodon
My Ativan
My IV
My Sudafed
She makes me feel good...uh!

I love waking up next to her
She is my Morning Star,
and the twinkle in her eye keeps me dazed for
days,
and I get high
So I travel to the second planet to understand

her a little better,
and there, I have conversations with God

to understand how she is made perfectly for
me
Because she always puts me first,
makes me feel like I am the last man on earth,
and my deity never ventures away from the
sun
She stays at home to take care of me,
so I will continue to be addicted to my
goddess
because I am in love...with her
And! She makes me feel good...uh!

She is my medicine
She is my medicine
She is my Geodon
My Ativan
My IV
My Sudafed
She makes me feel good...uh!

Some things in life

you can control.

But for the things you can't

do like Rev. Mase says,

"Breathe

Stretch

Shake

Let it go"

I Don't Live in a Box

I don't live in a box
   No, I am Free
I don't live in a box
   No, I am Free

      I don't live inside of a box
         I don't live inside of a box
      I don't live inside of a box

So you can trap me and confine me
      in a space
   where my limits are restricted or imprisoned
Where my mind is psychologically fenced in
               I will not be held captive
         I make my own choices
      I make my own decisions
   Because I am Free
Free from all the things
   that binds me to society
      Who set imaginary limitations
         and invisible boundaries
      I am free, because I live inside of me

I don't live in a box

No, I am Free
I don't live in a box
No, I am Free

You can't control me
Go ahead put me in jail
Cell block one fourteen
Take away my identity
Label me as number 645143
You see, your physical entrapment
allows me to be free
By providing the time
to grow spiritually
By finding myself
and asking who am I
When society doesn't allow us the time
In the meanwhile feeding us constant lies
Pushing us farther away
from our true purpose and potential
What hurts me is to see
Entrepreneurs taught to be drug dealers
Leaders taught to be gangsters
Models taught to be prostitutes
Society tells us who we are
But I challenge you to find the truth
You choose to be what you are taught
But I...

I don't live in a box
    No, I am Free
I don't live in a box
    No, I am Free

Road to the Final Four

-*Syracuse Men's and Women's 2016 Basketball Team Dedication*

It is very seldom
that opportunity meets chemistry and
greatness
with one thing in mind

One team
One goal

And as the story unfolds on the road to the
Final Four
The truth will be told
We are observing Kings and Queens
Dancing on a champion's playground
Where dreams become a reality
You do not want to intervene!
Defying gravity
Shooting ball with the stars
There are no limitations
Only one destination

the Final Four

I'll Never Forget

I can still remember
the first day we met
like it was yesterday.
How could I ever forget
your light green eyes,
your pearl white smile,
and your soft skin baby face.
I mean I knew I had to stop by
and drop a few lines,
even though I do admit
I was intimidated
by your sophisticated and intelligent style,
but to my surprise
you were attracted to my sexy smile.
So I sat down,
and instantly we clicked
like we were best friends
After only two weeks
you were my woman
and I was your man
After only a year
we were so deep in love
A love that was incredible
so indescribable that words are useless

A love so strong
it makes Webster look stupid
and cupid couldn't comprehend
Sometimes I used to ask myself
how did an angel fall into my hands.
An independent woman
who stood by her man's side,
and when I looked into your eyes
I knew I wanted to be with you
for the rest of my life
But I never imagined
I would be standing
next to you in a church
And I never imagined
when I leaned over
to give you a kiss
how much it would hurt
And I never imagined
I would cry so much
when they carried you to the hearse
And I never imagined
I would ever see my fiancée
lying six feet under dirt.
Why!
Why Lord!
Why did you do this to me?
I go to church
I pay my tithes

and I love you unconditionally
How dare you show me love
and take it away
What did I do to deserve this?
Are you punishing me?

Suddenly, as I am crying over your grave
an angel appeared to explain
Weep no more
for she is in a better place
It is not about you
It is according to his plan
and you must understand
You all have a purpose
and her purpose was
to make you a better man

I ate poetry for breakfast
two loafs of pages
filled with delicious juicy words.
Now what should I have for lunch?

Ms. Lady

Excuse me Ms. Lady
   I have been watching you for a while
   and I must say
Your beauty is unbelievably flawless
   Your attitude is overly sexy
   And your walk is like damn
It would be my honor
   if I could just hold your hand
   and get a chance to know you a lil bit
Because it is a privilege
   just being in your presence
   around your essence
You are
   by far
   the finest thing in the room
         and even though she's fine too
         "I want you"

Only Time Will Tell

I wish you could lie in my arms forever
however it's only an hour
before we depart
and I know it is hard
for my heart to bear
but the time we share
in these few moments
are priceless
because this hour
seems like only seconds
and these seconds
seem like a lifetime
I wish I can
turn back the hands of time
and place it on pause
because after all
time is the one
pushing me away from you

She told me she loves me
  that's all I needed to hear.

Romans 10, 9-13

"I am just a nobody
trying to tell everybody
about somebody
who can save anybody"

Let me tell you about my King
He reigns from heaven to earth
He died for all of our sins
and all of our kids
so we can live an eternal life.
He can save anybody
and solve every problem
He's that check in the mail
when you're down to your last dime
And check this!
He might not come when you want,
but He is right on time.
When your problems are over your head
and you want things to end
so you put that gun to your head
and play Russian roulette
with six bullets
but He is that gun
that jammed
because God said,

"No weapon formed against me
shall prosper
no, it won't work"

No matter who you are
or what you've done
He's ready to save
each and everyone
even if you have back slid
because He knows how tough it gets
being christian with temptation
Let's not forget
Job fell seven times
Remember

"For a saint is just a sinner
who fell down, and got up"

So all you have to do is
repent of all your sins,
confess Jesus as your savior,
be baptized in Jesus Christ,
and He will bless you
with an abundant life
He will open up the gates of heaven,
and accept you as his child
But again, who am I

Well, "I am just a nobody
trying to tell everybody
about somebody
who can save anybody"

Singles Ad

I'm looking for a woman
    Not just any type of woman
    but an independent woman

A woman who knows what she wants
but still stands by her man's side
A woman who can open up her own doors
but still lets me be a gentleman sometimes
    An independent woman
who doesn't always expect me to front the bill
but pushes my hand back
and says, "baby, I got this one here"
Not one of those Destiny Child type independent
women
who doesn't think they need a man
but one of those independent women
who doesn't need a man
but knows she needs a man
to fulfill her emotional feeling

I'm looking for a woman
    Not just any type of woman
    but a spiritual woman

A woman who puts God first

and knows she is nothing without Him
        A spiritual woman who wants me to go to
church
but doesn't complain when I don't go with her
A woman who likes to sing in the choir
Not one of those crazy spiritual type women
who thinks they are holier than thou
but one of those spiritual women
who's helping God save lives

I'm looking for a woman
        Not just any type of woman
        but a single woman

A woman who believes in monogamy
because she knows how beautiful being in love can be
        A single woman who wants to build a family
Not one of those off and on single type women
with those crazy ex-boyfriends stalking them
but one of those single women
who only got enough love for one man

I'm looking for a woman
        Not just any type of woman
        but a freaky woman

A woman who is not afraid of being exotic
and is very confident in her sexuality
        A woman who wants to fulfill her man's
fantasies

Not one of those extreme freaky type women
who likes having sex with multiple partners
But a freaky woman
who likes experimenting my body as well as hers

I'm looking for a woman
Not just any type of woman
but an independent, spiritual, single, freaky type woman
So ladies if you fit in that category
          please come holla at me
          I'm looking for a woman

Nature Rises

We make love like the sunset

You accept me into your waters

Causing the wind to blow

gently

onto your waves

Constantly flowing

Bouncing off the shore

And as the rays reflect

upon your surface

I travel deep

deep

deep inside you

until I fall asleep

and awake

the next morning

Superman

When people look at me!
They see a fighter and survivor
but I wonder if they see
the pain and frustration
that is burning deep in my soul
I...am...not...Superman!
No longer will I live up to your standards
Be defined by your rules and expectations
Try to fit in your groups
No! Not me
Because I am made of a different breed
If can't accept me for who I am
It is Okay!
I will stand alone,
and be marked as an outlaw
because you can't measure the size of my heart, or
determine what I am worth
I am great,
despite of what you think of me
How dare you have the audacity to tell me
that I am not good enough
Just walk...

walk a mile in my shoes,
and you will understand
my soles have been eroded from the concrete,
and I am actually walking barefooted,
but I leave no excuses to walk the next mile,
and while you continue to live life through my dreams
I will continue to be me
Giving a 110% percent of everything I do
because I choose to use my failures as experience,
and my setbacks as stepping-stones...
I will climb this mountain alone if I have to.
LOVE ME FOR WHO I AM!
And remove those kryptonite glasses
and you will see that I Am Superman!

I want to love you like an octopus,
with all three hearts.

A Marriage Well-Done

The most beautiful thing in the world
    is to be in love
  when two people
    are joined together as one
    mind, body, and soul
a man and a woman
    perfectly made for each other
When love goes far beyond
    physical attraction
a love that is intertwined
    with a spiritual connection
    and intellectual conservation
    lyrically flowing on one accord
    mentally falling in love
    with all of their strengths
    and all of their flaws
falling in love with self
    because they become one
a work of God's creation
        A marriage well-done

I had it Rough

I really thought
I had it rough growing up
living in the project
for over 20 years
having a single mom
breaking her back to pay the bills.
Most Christmases
we found it hard to smile
because Santa Claus
just flew over house half the time
and to top it off
I was born as a bastard child.
Never realizing I have my daddy's eyes
still figuring out who I am inside
and I always feel like
a piece of my puzzle is missing
because I haven't even seen the man in pictures

Yeah, I thought I had it rough
until I heard the next man's story
which made me feel like I was blessed

He was conceived from a rape victim
His mom's parents were Christian

and didn't believe in abortion,
so she decided to keep him
He developed all of his father's features,
so she decided to beat him
each time she had flashbacks
punishing him for his father's attack.
Torn in the middle of his heart
because he hated and loved them both
But then he said

Yeah, I thought I had it rough
until I heard the next girl's story
which made me feel like I was blessed

She was placed in a trash bag
Thrown in the nearest garbage can.
Left to die,
but she survived
Only to be moved from foster to foster home
left alone
with dirty old men
trying to take her innocence.
You see, she had to grow up way before her time
just to protect herself
because she had nobody else
But then she said

Yeah, I thought I had it rough
until I heard the your story
which made me feel like I was blessed

We must understand
we all have the same problems
just different situations and different outcomes.
You may not be able to control the cards
you are dealt,
but you most certainly can control the results.
Someone once said,
"10% of life is what happens to you
90% is how you respond to it."
Choose to be blessed!

It's funny how
time stops for no one

And the earth is constantly
spinning on its axis

But somehow
you managed to have time to slow down

And actually wait for
you

Boys & Girls Club of Jackson County

My career
started in 1992
When the doors opened to my foundation
My life
stands on pillows of multiple beating hearts
pumping blood into veins of determination and drive.
My success
is owed to the Boys & Girls Club of Jackson County
for having a vision to serve at-risk youths from the
    streets and to provide a place of need and purpose.
I was only 14
when those doors opened in Charles Warner Projects
My hood
wasn't all bad
just misguided souls
never been told or taught how to live life.
Some never exposed to love
Only mimicking images learned on the streets
The Boys & Girls Club was exactly what we needed.
Another place we could call home,
and for some kids it was the only place they cared
    enough to call home.

I can only remember maybe three of my teachers from
    elementary to high school
but I can remember each and every coordinator
who touched my life at the Boys & Girls Club
Cat, Jennifer, Snow, John, Iola, Denise, Thomas, Dee,
    Bernastein, Mrs. Dixon, Chico, Angie, and Beeve.
They are all pieces to the puzzle of me
When I look back on it
I went from being soft-spoken, timid,
and scared to open my mouth for what I wanted
to having courage, confidence,
and demanding nothing less but the very best for
    myself.
So I proudly spread my wings throughout this journey
    called life
because I know the wind will always be there to support
    me
And for that, I promise to always turn my head back like
    the Sankofa
to give back what was given to me
A dream of a new reality!

Hospital for Ex-Fighters

He laid his life on the line
for four years and 6 months.
He served his country well
but now he stands here in solitary confinement
between these four walls
treated like a disease.
His friends are the only ones who understand him
Ivan, the IV
and Willie, the wheelchair
Who have been here since his first day.
And he talks to them
through this small square they call a window
trying to avoid the writing on the wall
that he will never be able to serve his country again.
His condition is polluting his mind
Wondering why... He couldn't just die on the
    battlefield.
Instead he lived
and is constantly reminded by an amputated leg
that he is not worthy
These walls have heard the same story for years,
and as history repeats itself and the floor collects dirty
    tears
His friends finally decide to tell him
"There have been many before you

and more to come
There is a sun out there
right outside this window,
waiting for you!"

Luck of the Irish
Green beer, white snow, orange pride
Reversed traffic light

Tipperary Hill

49

Work for Change

He stood on the corner of Saint Mary and
Joseph's street
Long hair, blue eyes
with a facial expression of hopelessness
wearing worn down timberland boots,
no socks, a pair of cut off corduroy pants, and a ripped
up Nike shirt
saying "just do it" on the front
as if it was motivation for the sign he was
holding
"I will work for change"
As people passed him by
you could see heaven in his eyes,
but people still turned their heads and despised
his existence.
We are missing the bigger picture
It is simple
We all need to work for change
Giving More Love!

You are the space
between the sun and the moon
during a solar eclipse...

Mysteriously hidden beauty

Dr. William Wasson

-National Intramural-Recreational Sports Association Founder

Dr. William Wasson,
you don't know me
but it seems as if I know you very well
as if your thoughts, beliefs, and philosophy rest in
    my mind
I have heard great things about you
Like the time you invited 21 African Americans to
    your home at Dillard University
to break bread and share ideas
to create a recipe for a legacy.
You know, New Orleans is the city of creole
    cuisine
I mean...
I can only image
you all ate well at your first meeting.
I can picture a table
decorated with food for the soul
a pot of gumbo full of equity, diversity, and
    inclusion
a salad dressed with health and well-being
French bread baked with leadership
and beignets covered with a global perspective
served with love for all sustainable communities

Dr. William Wasson
I wish...I had...a breath...of your time
to ask
Did you know, in 1950, that you would create a
    movement?
Building mentors on top of mentors...in cycles
Creating a network of supportive colleagues that
    eventually become family
Opening doors and opportunities
Did you know...that you would create a career for
    me?
You developed leaders to develop me to develop
    leaders
and I know you would be proud
You would be proud of this association
for using your recipe to create trends, programs,
    and new facilities
to serve the campus communities
These core competencies for collegiate recreation
    are amazing
and it's crazy, how we serve this association
    unselfishly
The members are a mirror image of your direction
humble, genuine, and a family
that is still coming together every year adding to
    your legacy

Dr. William Wasson
I need you to know
that Momma Wasson

is still as beautiful as the first day you laid eyes on
    her.
She is nurturing leaders to follow in your footsteps

Greatness...is a hard act to follow
but our presidents stand on your shoulders
lifting this association to the top
providing education and development
for all professionals and student members

Dr. William Wasson,
Thank you for passing down your recipe
so we can break bread and share ideas
with...our...NIRSA...family

Social Media

Facebook Page – Seneca The Motivational Poet
Twitter - @SenecaTMPoet
Instagram - @SenecaTMPoet
YouTube – Seneca The Motivational Poet
SoundCloud – SenecaTMPoet

SenecaTMPoet.com

www.ingramcontent.com/pod-product-compliance
Lightning Source LLC
Chambersburg PA
CBHW071733020426
42331CB00008B/2005